I Feel...
ANXIOUS

Words and pictures by

DJ Corchin

Sometimes I feel **anxious** because of what people say.

Like when I hear **adults argue...**

and I'm not sure it's **OK.**

Or when there's a **germ** in the air

and I can't go and **play.**

Bad thoughts stick in my **head** and they won't go away.

Sometimes I feel **nervous** that I just won't fit in.

That no one will **pick** me on their team for the win.

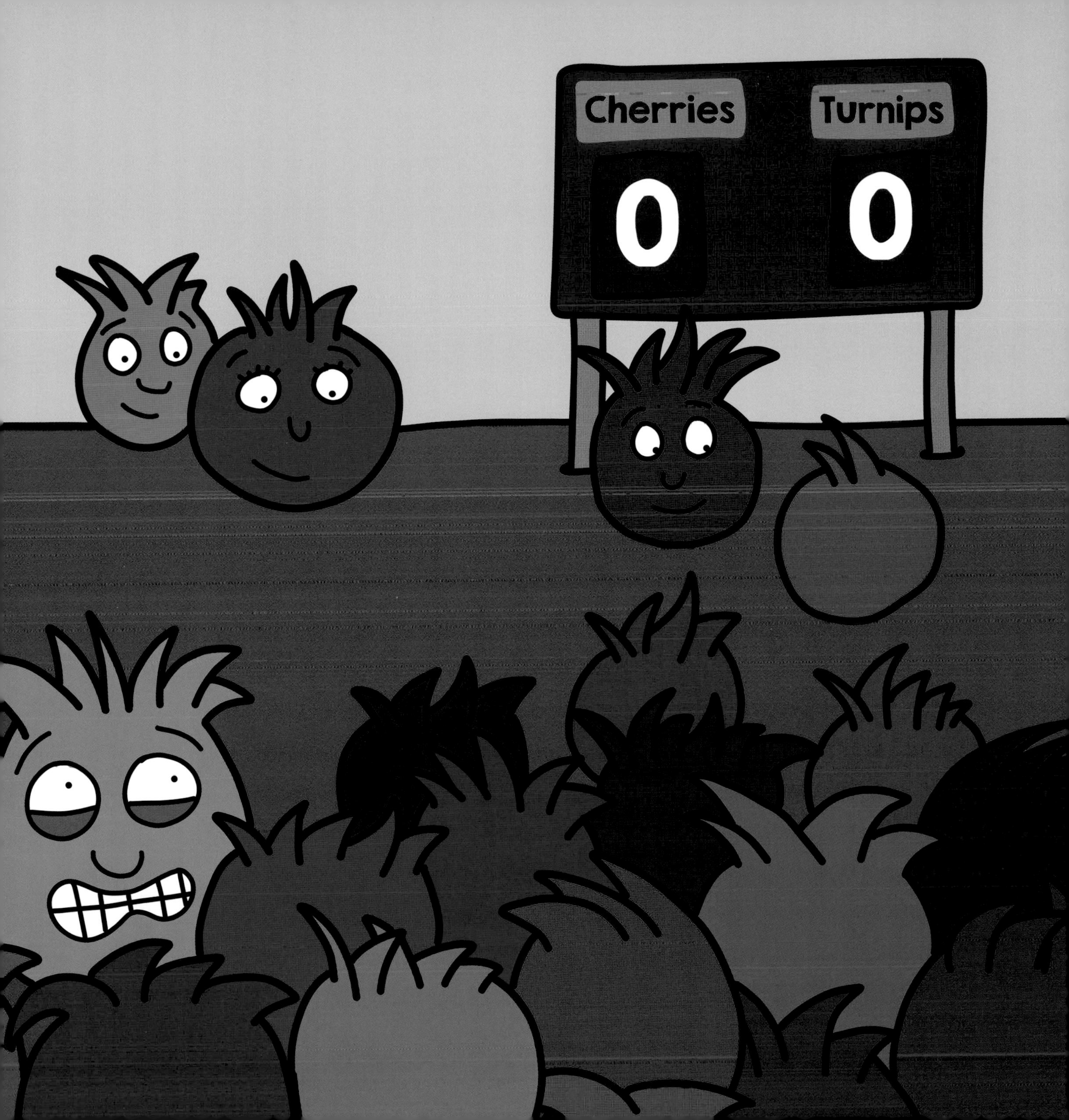
Cherries
Turnips
0
0

Or that people might **judge** me

on the shade of my skin.

It's hard to make **sense** of my feelings within.

Sometimes I'm on **edge**

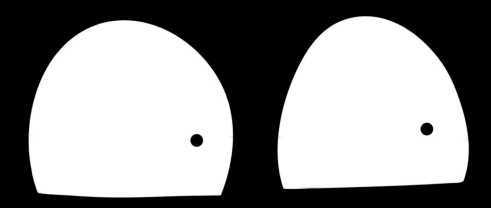

because someone turned
out the light.

Or they made a loud noise
and I jumped up in **fright**.

I'm really not **fond** of incredible heights.

So I try to **calm** down before I go on a flight.

I might take a deep **breath**

and think of a **magical** place.

I might **talk** to a friend,

or find my own **space**.

I can slow down my **thoughts** and take my own pace.

Or try something **fun**,

like **compete** in a race.

When that bug in my tummy
buzzes with fear,

and I know that my **feelings** are super unclear,

I'll take **one** step at a time,
and think of where to **begin**...

to come up with a plan
when I feel **anxious** within.

I Feel...
ANXIOUS

What's going to happen? What was that? Why is that happening? I'm so anxious!

Life can be pretty unpredictable. Not knowing what comes next or what is going to happen can make you feel nervous, worried, and anxious. Sometimes you feel so anxious you start to get scared. There are lots of things you can do to help when you're feeling anxious and those butterflies in your tummy just won't go away. Here's a few to start with!

Make an Anxious Meter

1. Cut a circle from cardboard or strong poster board about 12 to 16 inches in diameter.

2. Using the circle as a guide, draw another circle on a piece of white paper the same size. Cut it out.

3. Using a ruler or straight edge, draw four lines across the diameter of the circle like a pie evenly spaced. This should leave you with eight spaces.

4. Color four spaces next to each other in the following order: green, yellow, pink, purple.

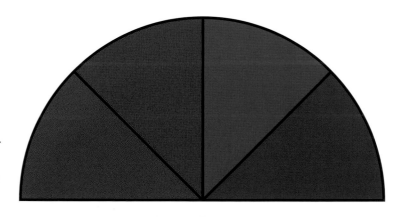

5. Once dried, label using a marker or pen as the following:

    Green – Not anxious, feeling great!

    Yellow – A little anxious and worried. Let's breathe!

    Pink – I'm anxious. Let's try my plan!*

    Purple – I'm very anxious and nervous. Let's find an adult and talk.

6. Glue the paper onto the thicker circle using a glue stick.

7. Cut off the bottom half of the circle, leaving just the other half with the colors and labels.

8. Attach a clothespin around the edge and move it to the space that indicates how you are currently feeling.

    *Your plan should be something you have worked out with a trusted adult that contains exercises, games, and activities you can use to calm yourself down when feeling anxious.

Are you afraid of what might happen or do you wonder what could?

Wonder or Fear?

Many times we're anxious because we think "What if something bad happens?" In any situation, there are a lot of things that can make us nervous if anything goes wrong. Often we forget about the things that could go right! Let's make a Wonder List of things we worry about and all the things that could be **AMAZING** if they happened.

1. Collect multiple sheets of 8.5½" x 11" paper, a marker or pen, and a ruler or straight edge.

2. On each sheet of paper, use the ruler and marker to draw two lines across the width of the paper (the short side), dividing the paper into three equal rectangles. You can do this on both sides of the paper.

3. In the top rectangle, write about something that makes you anxious when you think about it. For example, write **"I'm anxious about...** going to a new school."

4. In the middle rectangle, write **I'm afraid...** For example, "I'm afraid no one will like me" or "I'm afraid I won't be able to see my old friends."

5. In the bottom rectangle, write something amazing that could happen instead. Start with the words **I wonder...** For example, "I wonder if I'll meet people who are just as into dinosaurs and robots as I am." Or, "I wonder if I can start writing pen pal letters to my old friends so we can get mail every week!"

You can do this any time you feel anxious about something and want to change how you think about it.

Make soooooo many mistakes!

1. With a friend, grab some paper and some colored pencils, crayons, or markers.

2. First, each of you should draw your own I Feel... face using this book as examples. But when you draw yours, make a lot of mistakes. Put an eye where the mouth should go, the mouth where there should be hair, and don't even think about coloring in the lines!

3. Now, each of you START to draw a new I Feel... face, for example by drawing just the outline of the face shape (a circle, a square, etc.) and one feature like an eye.

4. Then pass the papers back and forth, each of you adding a feature and making a different mistake each time.

5. When you're all done, have fun talking about the silly things you created and seeing how sometimes making mistakes can turn into something fun and silly.

It is ALWAYS OK to ask someone for help when you are feeling bad.

The I Feel... Children's Series is a resource created to assist in discussions about emotional awareness.

Please seek the help of a trained mental healthcare professional and start a discussion today.

To Laura

Published by Sourcebooks eXplore, an imprint of Sourcebooks Kids
P.O. Box 4410, Naperville, Illinois 60567-4410
(630) 961-3900
sourcebookskids.com

Library of Congress Cataloging-in-Publication Data is on file with the publisher.

Source of Production: 1010 Printing Asia Limited, North Point, Hong Kong, China
Date of Production: December 2020
Run Number: 5020164

Printed and bound in China.
OGP 10 9 8 7 6 5 4 3 2 1